JAVA

DESIGN

PATTERNS

By

Devendra Singh

PREFACE

This technical e-book provides information about design patterns in java in the simplest way to understand. It consists of detailed descriptions of each Java design patterns with the simplest real world examples. All examples given in this e-book have been compiled & run by me in my development environment. I tried my best to have the simplest example available in this book.

This book is intended for java developers as a beginner or experienced. Any java developer can get benefits if he/she go through the full content & provided examples. I have written this book keeping in mind that every level of developer can get benefits from this.

Motivation for writing this e-book comes from the time I was learning java design patterns. It was not very easy to understand each and every pattern in one or two readings. I went through the various books & materials on the same and tried to extract relevant facts about the different patterns to make them understand easily & quickly. I have included all those relevant & crucial points in this book.

Before getting started I would like to introduce myself. I am a java developer having more than 10 years' experience in Java/J2EE technologies. Currently I am working with a multinational software company. One of my hobbies is to write technical contents. I spared some time to write this book & feeling very happy to share my experience and knowledge with other developers. In case you have any suggestion, correction or queries going through this e-book please don't hesitate to connect me on _erdsingh24@gmail.com_

At the last but not the least I would like to thank my parents for encouraging me to write this book.

Table of Contents

ABOUT DESIGN PATTERNS

If a problem occurs over and over again, a solution to that problem has been used effectively. That solution is described as a pattern. The design patterns are language-independent strategies for solving common object-oriented design problems. When you make a design, you should know the names of some common solutions. Learning design patterns is good for people to communicate each other effectively. In fact, you may have been familiar with some design patterns; you may not use well-known names to describe them. SUN suggests GOF (Gang of Four--four pioneer guys who wrote a book named "Design Patterns"- Elements of Reusable Object-Oriented Software), so we use that book as our guide to describe solutions. Please make you be familiar with these terms and learn how other people solve the coding problems.

If you want to be a professional Java developer, you should know at least some popular solutions to coding problems. Such solutions have been proved efficient and effective by the experienced developers. These solutions are described as so-called design patterns. Learning design patterns speeds up your experience accumulation in OOA/OOD. Once you grasped them, you would be benefitted from them for all your life and jump up yourselves to be a master of designing and developing. Furthermore, you will be able to use these terms to communicate with your fellows or assessors more effectively.

Many programmers with many years' experience don't know design patterns, but as an Object-Oriented programmer, you have to know them well, especially for new Java programmers. Actually, when you solved a coding problem, you have used a design pattern. You may not use a popular name to describe it or may not choose an effective way to better intellectually control over what you built. Learning how the experienced developers to solve the coding problems and trying to use them in your project are a best way to earn your experience and certification.

Remember that learning the design patterns will really change how you design your code; not only will you be smarter but will you sound a lot smarter, too. The 23 design patterns by GOF are well known, and more are to be discovered on the way.

There are three well-known types of design patterns.

Creational Design Patterns: Creational design patterns provide solution to instantiate an object in the best possible way for specific situations. Following design patterns come under this category.

> *Singleton Pattern
> * Factory Pattern
> * Abstract Factory Pattern
> * Builder Pattern
> * Prototype Pattern

Structural Design Patterns: Structural patterns provide different ways to create a class structure, for example using inheritance and composition to create a large object from small objects. Following design patterns come under this category.

> * Adapter Pattern
> * Composite Pattern
> * Proxy Pattern
> * Flyweight Pattern
> * Facade Pattern
> * Bridge Pattern
> * Decorator Pattern

Behavioral Design Patterns: Behavioral patterns provide solution for the better interaction between objects and how to provide lose coupling and flexibility to extend easily. Following design patterns come under this category.

* Template Method Pattern
* Mediator Pattern
* Chain of Responsibility Pattern
* Observer Pattern
* Strategy Pattern
* Command Pattern
* State Pattern
* Visitor Pattern
* Iterator Pattern
* Interpreter Pattern
* Memento Pattern

SINGLETON PATTERN

Sometimes it's important for some classes to have exactly one instance. There are many objects we only need one instance of them and if we, instantiate more than one, we'll run into all sorts of problems like incorrect program behavior, overuse of resources, or inconsistent results.

There are only two points in the definition of a singleton design pattern,

> * There should be only one instance allowed for a class and

> * We should allow global point of access to that single instance.

From the definition, it seems to be a very simple design pattern but when it comes to implementation, it comes with a lot of implementation concerns. The implementation of Java Singleton **pattern has always** been a controversial topic among developers. Here we will learn about Singleton design pattern principles, different ways to implement Singleton design pattern and some of the best practices for its usage.

Lazy initialization will be beneficial when we want to delay the initialization until it is not needed. because if we use eager initialization and if initialization fails there is no chance to get the instance further while in lazy initialization we may get it in second chance. In Lazy initialization we will not get instance until we call getInstance () method while in eager initialization it creates instance at the time of class loading.

There are some examples where Singleton pattern violation situation can be found.
We will compare the hash code values of the objects to verify the similar objects. If hash code values of two objects are equal, those objects must be equal.

* **Reflection:** Using reflection we can set the private constructor to become accessible at runtime as shown in the example below.

```java
import java.lang.reflect.Constructor;

public class SingletonR {

    private static SingletonR instance=new SingletonR();

    private SingletonR(){
        System.out.println("Creating...");

    }

    public static SingletonR getInstance(){
        return instance;
    }

    public static void main(String[] args) throws Exception {
        SingletonR s1= SingletonR.getInstance();
        SingletonR s2= SingletonR.getInstance();

        print("s1",s1);
        print("s2",s2);

        Class clazz= Class.forName("com.dev.dp.creational.singleton.SingletonR");
        Constructor<SingletonR> ctor= clazz.getDeclaredConstructor();
        ctor.setAccessible(true);
        SingletonR s3=ctor.newInstance();

        print("s3",s3);
    }

    static void print(String name, SingletonR obj){
        System.out.println(String.format("Object : %s, Hashcode: %d",name,obj.hashCode()));
    }
}
```

Output:

```
Creating...
Object : s1, Hashcode: 31168322
Object : s2, Hashcode: 31168322
Creating...
Object : s3, Hashcode: 17225372
```

How to fix: Throw Runtime Exception if someone tries to make instance in case one instance already exists. This code will go into the private constructor of the Singleton class.

```
private SingletonR(){
    System.out.println("Creating...");
    if(instance != null){
        throw new RuntimeException("can't create instance. Please use getinstance()");
    }
}
```

Output post fix:

```
Creating...
Object : s1, Hashcode: 31168322
Object : s2, Hashcode: 31168322
Creating...
Exception in thread "main" java.lang.reflect.InvocationTargetException
        at sun.reflect.NativeConstructorAccessorImpl.newInstance0(Native Method)
        at sun.reflect.NativeConstructorAccessorImpl.newInstance(Unknown Source)
        at sun.reflect.DelegatingConstructorAccessorImpl.newInstance(Unknown Source)
        at java.lang.reflect.Constructor.newInstance(Unknown Source)
        at com.dev.dp.creational.singleton.SingletonR.main(SingletonR.java:33)
Caused by: java.lang.RuntimeException: can't create instance. Please use getinstance()
        at com.dev.dp.creational.singleton.SingletonR.<init>(SingletonR.java:15)
        ... 5 more
```

* Cloning: If we try to make instance by cloning it, the generated hash code of cloned copy doesn't **match** with the actual object so it also violates the Singleton principle.

```
public class SingletonC implements Cloneable{

    private static SingletonC instance=new SingletonC();

    private SingletonC(){
        System.out.println("Creating...");

    }

    public static SingletonC getInstance(){
        return instance;
    }

    @Override
    protected Object clone() throws CloneNotSupportedException{
    //  if(instance !=null) throw new CloneNotSupportedException();
        return super.clone();
    }

    public static void main(String[] args) throws Exception {
        SingletonC s1= SingletonC.getInstance();
        SingletonC s2= SingletonC.getInstance();

        print("s1",s1);
        print("s2",s2);

        SingletonC s3= (SingletonC)s2.clone();

        print("s3",s3);
    }

    static void print(String name, SingletonC obj){
        System.out.println(String.format("Object : %s, Hashcode: %d",name,obj.hashCode()));
    }
}
```

Output:

```
Creating...
Object : s1, Hashcode: 31168322
Object : s2, Hashcode: 31168322
Object : s3, Hashcode: 17225372
```

How to fix: Throw CloneNotSupportedException from the clone () method if someone tries to make other instance of it. Uncomment the commented line from clone () method.

Output post fix:

```
Creating...
Object : s1, Hashcode: 31168322
Object : s2, Hashcode: 31168322
Exception in thread "main" java.lang.CloneNotSupportedException
        at com.dev.dp.creational.singleton.SingletonC.clone(SingletonC.java:18)
        at com.dev.dp.creational.singleton.SingletonC.main(SingletonC.java:29)
```

* Serialization/Deserialization: When we serialize an object and deserialize it again there are different hash code values generated as shown in the example below. So our Singleton principle breaks in case of object serialization/deserialization.

```java
import java.io.FileInputStream;□

public class SingletonS implements Serializable{

    private static SingletonS instance=new SingletonS();

    private SingletonS(){
        System.out.println("Creating...");
    }

    public static SingletonS getInstance(){
        return instance;
    }

    public static void main(String[] args) throws Exception {
        SingletonS s1= SingletonS.getInstance();
        SingletonS s2= SingletonS.getInstance();

        print("s1",s1);
        print("s2",s2);

        ObjectOutputStream oos = new ObjectOutputStream(new FileOutputStream("/tmp/s2.ser"));
        oos.writeObject(s2);

        ObjectInputStream ois= new ObjectInputStream(new FileInputStream("/tmp/s2.ser"));
        SingletonS s3 =(SingletonS)ois.readObject();
        print("s3",s3);|
    }

    static void print(String name, SingletonS obj){
        System.out.println(String.format("Object : %s, Hashcode: %d",name,obj.hashCode()));
    }
}
```

Output:

```
Creating...
Object : s1, Hashcode: 31168322
Object : s2, Hashcode: 31168322
Object : s3, Hashcode: 6585861
```

How to Fix: Implement readResolve () method in the Singleton class as shown below.

```java
private Object readResolve(){
    System.out.println("applying read resolve...");
    return instance;
}
```

Output post fix:

```
Creating...
Object : s1, Hashcode: 31168322
Object : s2, Hashcode: 31168322
applying read resolve...
Object : s3, Hashcode: 31168322
```

* Multithreaded: Singleton will work properly in
multithreaded environment only if eager instantiation
has been done because in this case instance creation will
happen at the time of class loading only. But for Lazy
instantiation we will have to take care of multiple things.
If we want to delay the instantiation because of cost, we
use to go with lazy.
Following code demonstrates the behavior of Singleton
instance when two threads are getting executed by
comparing their hash code values. Be careful while
running the following code as it will work only in Java 8
and later versions.

```java
public class SingletonT {

    private static SingletonT instance=null; //lazy initialization

    private SingletonT(){
        System.out.println("Creating...");
    }

    public static SingletonT getInstance(){
        if (instance == null) {
            instance = new SingletonT();
        }
        return instance;
    }

    static void useSingleton(){
        SingletonT singleton = SingletonT.getInstance();
        print("singleton",singleton);
    }

    public static void main(String[] args) throws Exception {
        ExecutorService service = Executors.newFixedThreadPool(2);
        service.submit(SingletonT::useSingleton);
        service.submit(SingletonT::useSingleton);
        service.shutdown();
    }

    static void print(String name, SingletonT obj){
        System.out.println(String.format("Object : %s, Hashcode: %d",name,obj.hashCode()));
    }
}
```

Output:

```
Creating...
Object : singleton, Hashcode: 14229844
Object : singleton, Hashcode: 14229844
```

When you run the above program many times you will notice that in multithreaded environment sometimes Singleton principle works but sometimes it violates. Therefore we need to synchronize the getInstance () method as shown below.

```
public static synchronized SingletonT getInstance(){
    if (instance == null) {
        instance = new SingletonT();
    }
    return instance;
}
```

After applying synchronize keyword in the getInstance () method the program will execute properly without any issue but in Java instead of synchronizing whole method we can synchronize only the block of code which is affected while creating instance to escape the extra overhead as below.

```
27    public static SingletonT getInstance(){
28        if (instance == null) {
29            synchronized (SingletonT.class) {
30                instance = new SingletonT();
31            }
32        }
33        return instance;
34    }
```

From the above code we have narrowed down the scope of synchronization for performance reasons. Notice that if a thread at line # 28 sees that instance is null and then it gets the lock of object at line # 29. At the same time if another thread already has the lock it will create the instance. So to make sure no other thread has already acquired the lock we will apply one more check after acquiring the lock as shown below. This method is called **Double Checked Locking.**

```
27   public static SingletonT getInstance() {
28       if (instance == null) { // check 1
29           synchronized (SingletonT.class) {
30               if (instance == null) { // check2
31                   instance = new SingletonT();
32               }
33           }
34       }
35       return instance;
36   }
```

Sometimes double checked locking also breaks the Principle of Singleton.

Java runtime publishes half initialized variable. Suppose 2 threads threa1 & thread2 are entering into the code it goes through the line # 28 to line # 31 and created the instance. At the same time thread 2 enters and it knows that there is something in variable named as 'instance' (since it is at half initialized state) and it returns the same from line # 35. Therefore Singleton principle breaks.

To address this situation use **volatile** keyword at the time of instance declaration. Value of volatile variable will be published only when the change completes. Change to write operation happens before read operation in volatile variable. In short all threads will see the same value of variable.

```
private static volatile SingletonT instance=null; //lazy initialization
```

* Holder Class (Bill Pugh Method): Bill Pugh came up with a different approach to create the Singleton class using an inner static helper class.

```
package com.dev.dp.creational.singleton;

public class SingletonH {

    private SingletonH(){
        System.out.println("Creating...");
    }

    static class Holder {
        static final SingletonH INSTANCE= new SingletonH();//lazy
    }

    public static SingletonH getInstance(){
        return Holder.INSTANCE;
    }

    public static void main(String[] args) throws Exception {
        SingletonH s1= SingletonH.getInstance();
        SingletonH s2= SingletonH.getInstance();
        SingletonH s3= SingletonH.getInstance();

        print("s1",s1);
        print("s2",s2);
        print("s3",s3);
    }

    static void print(String name, SingletonH obj){
        System.out.println(String.format("Object : %s, Hashcode: %d",name,obj.hashCode()));
    }
}
```

```
Creating...
Object : s1, Hashcode: 31168322
Object : s2, Hashcode: 31168322
Object : s3, Hashcode: 31168322
```

* Enum Singleton: Joshua Bloch suggests the use of Enum to implement Singleton design pattern as Java ensures that any enum value is instantiated only once in a Java program. Since Java Enum values are globally accessible, so is the singleton. The drawback is that the enum type is somewhat inflexible; for example, it does not allow lazy initialization.

```
package com.dev.dp.creational.singleton;

public enum EnumSingleton {

    INSTANCE;

    public static void doSomething() {
        // do something
    }
}
```

Enum Singleton doesn't violate principle of Singleton in any case described above.

FACTORY PATTERN

Factory design pattern is used when we have a super class with multiple sub-classes and based on input, we need to return one of the sub-classes. This pattern takes out the responsibility of instantiation of a class from client program to the factory class. We can apply Singleton pattern on Factory class or make the factory method static.

Super class in factory pattern can be an interface or a normal java class.

Benefits:

* Factory pattern provides approach to code for interface rather than implementation.
* Factory pattern removes the instantiation of actual implementation classes from client code, making it more robust, less coupled and easy to extend. For example, we can easily change PC class implementation because client program is unaware of this.
* Factory pattern provides abstraction between implementation and client classes through inheritance.

Usage in JDK:

* java.util.Calendar, ResourceBundle and NumberFormat getInstance () methods uses Factory pattern.
* valueOf () method in wrapper classes like Boolean, Integer etc.

```
package com.dev.dp.creational.factory;
public interface IMobile {
    public void cost();
    public void pictureCapacity();
    public void batteryPower();
}
```

```java
public class Lenovo implements IMobile{

    @Override
    public void cost() {
        System.out.println("Lenovo Cost starts from 10000");
    }

    @Override
    public void pictureCapacity() {
        System.out.println("Lenovo camera capacity starts from 10 MP");
    }

    @Override
    public void batteryPower() {
        System.out.println("Lenovo battery power starts from 2500 MAh");
    }

    @Override
    public String toString() {
        return "Lenovo [toString()=" + super.toString() + "]";
    }

}


public class Samsung implements IMobile {

    @Override
    public void cost() {
        System.out.println("Samsung Cost starts from 6000");
    }

    @Override
    public void pictureCapacity() {
        System.out.println("Samsung camera capacity starts from 4 MP");
    }

    @Override
    public void batteryPower() {
        System.out.println("Samsung battery power starts from 1200 MAh");
    }

}
```

```java
package com.dev.dp.creational.factory;

public class MobileFactory {

    public MobileFactory(){

    }

    IMobile createMobile(String type){

        IMobile mob=null;
        if("len".equalsIgnoreCase(type)){
            mob=new Lenovo();
            System.out.println("Lenovo created");
        }else if("sam".equalsIgnoreCase(type)){
            mob=new Samsung();
            System.out.println("Samsung created");
        }
        return mob;
    }
}
```

```java
public class FactoryTest {

    public static void main(String[] args) {
        MobileFactory factory= new MobileFactory();

        Lenovo len = (Lenovo)factory.createMobile("len");
        len.batteryPower();

        Samsung sam= (Samsung)factory.createMobile("sam");
        sam.cost();
    }
}
```

Output:

```
Lenovo created
Lenovo battery power starts from 2500 MAh
Samsung created
Samsung Cost starts from 6000
```

<u>Other Example:</u> Animal: Dog, Cat, Fox etc.

ABSTRACT FACTORY PATTERN

Almost similar to except the fact that it's more like
factory of factories. If you are familiar with factory design
pattern in java, you will notice that we have a single
Factory class that returns the different sub-classes based

on the input provided and factory class uses if-else or switch statement to achieve this. In Abstract Factory pattern, we get rid of if-else block and have a factory class for each sub-class and then an Abstract Factory class that will return the sub-class based on the input factory class.

An abstract factory is a factory that returns factories. Why is this layer of abstraction useful? A normal factory can be used to create sets of related objects. An abstract factory returns factories. Thus, an abstract factory is used to return factories that can be used to create sets of related objects.

As an example, you could have a Honda factory that returns car objects (Brio, Civic, etc.) associated with a Honda factory. You could also have a Hyundai factory that returns car objects (Santro, EON) associated with a Hyundai factory. We could create an abstract factory that returns these different types of car factories depending on the car that we were interested in. We could then obtain car objects from the car factories. Via polymorphism, we can use a common interface to get the different factories, and we could then use a common interface to get the different cars.

Benefits:

* Abstract Factory pattern provides approach to code for interface rather than implementation.

* Abstract Factory pattern is "factory of factories" and can be easily extended to accommodate more products, for example we can add another sub-class Celerio and a factory MarutiFactory.

* Abstract Factory pattern is robust and avoid conditional logic of Factory pattern.

Usage in JDK:

*
javax.xml.parsers.DocumentBuilderFactory#newInstance()
*
javax.xml.transform.TransformerFactory#newInstance()

* javax.xml.xpath.XPathFactory#newInstance()

When to use: A family of related product objects is designed to be used together, and you need to enforce this constraint.

```
package com.dev.dp.creational.abstractFactory;

public interface IMobileFactory {

    IMobileFactory createMobile(String type);
}
```

```java
public class MobileFactory implements IMobileFactory {

    @Override
    public IMobileFactory createMobile(String type) {
        IMobileFactory mob = null;
        if ("lenf".equalsIgnoreCase(type)){
            mob= new LenovoMobileFactory();
        } else if ("samf".equalsIgnoreCase(type)){
            mob= new SamsungMobileFactory();
        }
        return mob;
    }

}
```

```java
public class LenovoMobileFactory extends MobileFactory {

    Lenovo createLenovoMobile(){
        return new Lenovo();
    }

}
```

```java
public class SamsungMobileFactory extends MobileFactory {

    Samsung createSamsungMobile(){
        return new Samsung();
    }
}
```

```java
public class AbstractFactoryTest {

    public static void main(String[] args) {
      MobileFactory factory= new MobileFactory();
      LenovoMobileFactory lmf= (LenovoMobileFactory)factory.createMobile("lenf");
      Lenovo ln= (Lenovo)lmf.createLenovoMobile();
      ln.pictureCapacity();
    }

}
```

Output:

```
Lenovo camera capacity starts from 10 MP
```

Other Example:

Honda Factory: Brio, Civic,

Hyundai Factory: Santro, EON etc.

BUILDER PATTERN

In general, the details of object construction, such as instantiating and initializing the components that make up the object, are kept within the object, often as part of its constructor. This type of design closely ties the object construction process with the components that make up the object. This approach is suitable as long as the object under construction is simple and the object construction process is definite and always produces the same representation of the object.

However, this design may not be effective when the object being created is complex and the series of steps constituting the object creation process can be implemented in different ways, thus producing different representations of the object. Because the different implementations of the construction process are all kept within the object, the object can become bulky (construction bloat) and less modular. Subsequently, adding a new implementation or making changes to an existing implementation requires changes to the existing code.

Using the Builder pattern, the process of constructing such an object can be designed more effectively. The Builder pattern suggests moving the construction logic out of the object class to a separate class referred to as a builder class.

There can be more than one such builder classes, each with different implementations for the series of steps to construct the object. Each builder implementation results in a different representation of the object.

The intent of the Builder Pattern is to separate the construction of a complex object from its representation, so that the same construction process can create different representations. This type of separation reduces the object size. The design turns out to be more modular with each implementation contained in a different builder object. Adding a new implementation (i.e., adding a new builder) becomes easier. The object construction process becomes independent of the components that make up the object. This provides more control over the object construction process.

The Builder pattern suggests using a dedicated object referred to as a Director, which is responsible for invoking different builder methods required for the construction of the final object. Different client objects can make use of the Director object to create the required object. Once the object is constructed, the client object can directly request from the builder the fully constructed object. To facilitate this process, a new method getObject () can be declared in the common Builder interface to be implemented by different concrete builders.

Builder
* Specifies an abstract interface for creating parts of a Product object.

ConcreteBuilder

* Constructs and assembles parts of the product by implementing the Builder interface.

* Defines and keeps track of the representation it creates.

* Provides an interface for retrieving the product.

Director

* Constructs an object using the Builder interface.

Product

* Represents the complex object under construction. ConcreteBuilder builds the product's internal representation and defines the process by which it's assembled.

* Includes classes that define the constituent parts, including interfaces for assembling the parts into the final result.

Example:

```
⊿ ⊞ com.dev.dp.creational.builder2
    ▷ Ⓙ BuilderTest.java
    ▷ Ⓙ IndianMealBuilder.java
    ▷ Ⓙ JapaneseMealBuilder.java
    ▷ Ⓙ Meal.java
    ▷ Ⓙ MealBuilder.java
    ▷ Ⓙ MealDirector.java
```

Another form of the Builder Pattern:

Sometimes there is an object with a long list of properties, and most of these properties are optional. Consider an online form which needs to be filled in order to become a member of a site. You need to fill all the mandatory fields but you can skip the optional fields or sometimes it may look valuable to fill some of the optional fields.

The question is, what sort of constructor should we write for such a class? Well writing a constructor with long list of parameters is not a good choice, this could frustrate the client especially if the important fields are only a few. This could increase the scope of error; the client may provide a value accidentally to a wrong field. Long sequences of identically typed parameters can cause subtle bugs. If the client accidentally reverses two such parameters, the compiler won't complain, but the program will misbehave at runtime.

Instead of making the desired object directly, the client calls a constructor with all of the required parameters and gets a builder object. Then the client calls setter-like methods on the builder object to set each optional parameter of interest. Finally, the client calls a parameterless build method to generate the object.

* First of all you need to create a static nested class and then copy all the arguments from the outer class to the Builder class. We should follow the naming convention and if the class name is Cake then builder class should be named as CakeBuilder.
* The Builder class should have a public constructor with all the required attributes as parameters.
* Builder class should have methods to set the optional parameters and it should return the same Builder object after setting the optional attribute.

* The final step is to provide a build () method in the builder class that will return the Object needed by client program. For this we need to have a private constructor in the Class with Builder class as argument.

```java
class Cake {
    private final double sugar;   //cup
    private final double butter;  //cup
    private final double milk;    //cup
    private final int cherry;

    public static class CakeBuilder {
        private double sugar;     //cup
        private double butter;    //cup
        private double milk;      //cup
        private int cherry;
        //builder methods for setting property
        public CakeBuilder sugar(double cup){this.sugar = cup; return this; }
        public CakeBuilder butter(double cup){this.butter = cup; return this; }
        public CakeBuilder milk(double cup){this.milk = cup; return this; }
        public CakeBuilder cherry(int number){this.cherry = number; return this; }
        //return fully build object
        public Cake build() {
            return new Cake(this);
        }
    }

    //private constructor to enforce object creation through builder
    private Cake(CakeBuilder builder) {
        this.sugar = builder.sugar;
        this.butter = builder.butter;
        this.milk = builder.milk;
        this.cherry = builder.cherry;
    }

    @Override
    public String toString() {
        return "Cake [sugar=" + sugar + ", butter=" + butter + ", milk=" + milk + ", cherry=" + cherry + "]";
    }
}
```

```java
public class BuilderPattern {

    public static void main(String[] args) {
        //Creating object using Builder pattern in java
        Cake whiteCake = new Cake.CakeBuilder().sugar(1).butter(0.5).milk(0.5).build();

        //Cake is ready to eat :)
        System.out.println(whiteCake);
    }

}
```

Output: Cake [sugar=1.0, butter=0.5, milk=0.5, cherry=0]

In static class setting property, we can use setter method as another option.

As you can clearly see, now a client only needs to provide the mandatory fields and the fields which are important to him. To create the form object now, we need invoke the CakeBuilder constructor which takes the mandatory fields and then we need to call the set of required methods on it and finally the build method to get the form object.

When to use the Builder Pattern:

Use the Builder pattern when
* The algorithm for creating a complex object should be independent of the parts that make up the object and how they're assembled.

* The construction process must allow different representations for the object that's constructed.

Builder Pattern in JDK:

* java.lang.StringBuilder#append() (unsynchronized)
* java.lang.StringBuffer#append() (synchronized)
* java.nio.ByteBuffer#put() (also on CharBuffer, ShortBuffer, IntBuffer, LongBuffer, FloatBuffer and DoubleBuffer)
* javax.swing.GroupLayout.Group#addComponent()
* All implementations of java.lang.Appendable.

PROTOTYPE PATTERN

Prototype pattern is one of the Creational Design patterns, so it provides a mechanism of object creation. Prototype pattern is used when the Object creation is a costly affair and requires a lot of time and resources and you have a similar object already existing. So this pattern provides a mechanism to copy the original object to a new object and then modify it according to our needs. This pattern uses java cloning to copy the object.

It would be easy to understand this pattern with an example, suppose we have an Object that loads data from database. Now we need to modify this data in our program multiple times, so it's not a good idea to create the Object using new keyword and load all the data again from database. So the better approach is to clone the existing object into a new object and then do the data manipulation. Prototype design pattern mandates that the Object which you are copying should provide the copying feature. It should not be done by any other class. However whether to use shallow or deep copy of the Object properties depends on the requirements and it's a design decision.

One example of how this can be useful is if an original object is created with a resource such as a data stream that may not be available at the time that a clone of the object is needed. Another example is if the original object creation involves a significant time commitment, such as reading data from a database or over a network.

Normally in Java, if you'd like to use cloning (i.e., the prototype pattern), you can utilize the clone () method and the Cloneable interface. By default, clone () performs a shallow copy. Serializable can be used to simplify deep copying.
However, we can implement our own prototype pattern. To do so, we'll create a Prototype interface that features a doClone () method.

Below example describes how to design an advanced bike after cloning the basic bike object.

```java
public class Bike implements Cloneable {

    private int gears;
    private String bikeType;
    private String model;

    public Bike() {
        bikeType="Standard";
        model= "Leopard";
        gears=4;
    }

    public Bike clone(){
        return new Bike();
    }

    public void makeAdvanced(){
        bikeType = "Advanced";
        model = "Jaguar";
        gears = 6;
    }

    public String getModel(){
        return model;
    }

    @Override
    public String toString() {
        return "Bike [gears=" + gears + ", bikeType="
              + bikeType + ", model=" + model + "]";
    }

}
```

```
public class PrototypeTest {

    public Bike makeJaguar(Bike basicBike){

        basicBike.makeAdvanced();
        return basicBike;
    }

    public static void main(String[] args) {

        Bike bike = new Bike();
        Bike basicBike=bike.clone();
        PrototypeTest pt = new PrototypeTest();
        Bike advancedBike= pt.makeJaguar(basicBike);
        System.out.println("Prototype Design Pattern: "+advancedBike.getModel());
        System.out.println("Prototype Design Pattern: "+advancedBike.toString());
    }

}
```

Output:

```
Prototype Design Pattern: Jaguar
Prototype Design Pattern: Bike [gears=6, bikeType=Advanced, model=Jaguar]
```

When to Use:

* When the classes to instantiate are specified at run-time, for example, by dynamic loading; or

* To avoid building a class hierarchy of factories that parallels the class hierarchy of products; or

* When instances of a class can have one of only a few different combinations of state. It may be more convenient to install a corresponding number of prototypes and clone them rather than instantiating the class manually, each time with the appropriate state.

ADAPTER PATTERN

Sometimes, there could be a scenario when two objects don't fit together, as they should in-order to get the work done. This situation could arise when we are trying to integrate a legacy code with a new code, or when changing a 3rd party API in the code. This is due to incompatible interfaces of the two objects which do not fit together.

In other words, **Adapter design pattern** is one of the **structural design patterns** and it's used so that two unrelated interfaces can work together. The object that joins these unrelated interfaces is called an **Adapter**. As a real life example, we can think of a mobile charger as an adapter because mobile battery needs 3 volts to charge but the normal socket produces either 120V (US) or 240V (India). So the mobile charger works as an adapter between mobile charging socket and the wall socket.

In the adapter pattern, a wrapper class (i.e., the adapter) is used translate requests from it to another class (i.e., the adoptee). In effect, an adapter provides particular interactions with an adoptee that are not offered directly by the adoptee.

The adapter pattern takes two forms. In the first form, a "class adapter" utilizes inheritance. The class adapter extends the adoptee class and adds the desired methods to the adapter. These methods can be declared in an interface (i.e., the "target" interface).In the second form; an "object adapter" utilizes composition. The object adapter contains an adoptee and implements the target interface to interact with the adoptee.

```java
public class Apple {

    public void getAppleColor(String color){
        System.out.println("Apple color is :"+color);
    }
}


public class Orange {

    public void getOrangeColor(String color){
        System.out.println("Orange color is :"+color);
    }
}


public class AppleAdapter extends Apple{
    //The purpose of the sample problem is to adapt an orange as an apple.
    private Orange orange;

    public AppleAdapter(Orange orange){
        this.orange = orange;
    }

    public void getColor(String color){
        orange.getOrangeColor(color);
    }
}
```

```
public class AdapterPatternTest {

    public static void main(String[] args) {

        Apple apple1 = new Apple();
        apple1.getAppleColor("green");

        Orange orange = new Orange();
        AppleAdapter adapter = new AppleAdapter(orange);
        adapter.getAppleColor("red");

    }

}
```

Output:

```
Apple color is :green
Apple color is :red
```

Orange is adoptee, apple is target & AppleAdapter is the adapter. Here idea is to pass adoptee in adapter's constructor to achieve the goal.

When to use Adapter Pattern:

The Adapter pattern should be used when:
* There is an existing class, and its interface does not match the one you need.

* You want to create a reusable class that cooperates with unrelated or unforeseen classes, that is, classes that don't necessarily have compatible interfaces.

* There are several existing subclasses to be use, but it's impractical to adapt their interface by subclassing every one. An object adapter can adapt the interface of its parent class.

Adapter Pattern Example in JDK:

* java.util.Arrays#asList()

* java.io.InputStreamReader(InputStream) (returns a Reader)

* java.io.OutputStreamWriter(OutputStream) (returns a Writer)

COMPOSITE PATTERN

There are times when you feel a need of a tree data structure in your code. There are many variations to the tree data structure, but sometimes there is a need of a tree in which both branches as well as leafs of the tree should be treated as uniformly.

The Composite Pattern allows you to compose objects into a tree structure to represent the part-whole hierarchy which means you can create a tree of objects that is made of different parts, but that can be treated as a whole one big thing. **Composite lets clients to treat individual objects**

and compositions of objects uniformly, that's the intent of the Composite Pattern.

In the composite pattern, a tree structure exists where identical operations can be performed on leaves and nodes. A node in a tree is a class that can have children. A node class is a 'composite' class. A leaf in a tree is a 'primitive' class that does not have children. The children of a composite can be leaves or other composites.

The leaf class and the composite class share a common 'component' interface that defines the common operations that can be performed on leaves and composites. When an operation on a composite is performed, this operation is performed on all children of the composite, whether they are leaves or composites. Thus, the composite pattern can be used to perform common operations on the objects that compose a tree.

In Other words, Composite Pattern consists of following objects.

Base Component – Base component is the interface for all objects in the composition, client program uses base component to work with the objects in the composition. It can be an interface or an abstract class with some methods common to all the objects.

Leaf – Defines the behavior for the elements in the composition. It is the building block for the composition and implements base component. It doesn't have references to other Components.

Composite – It consists of leaf elements and implements the operations in base component.

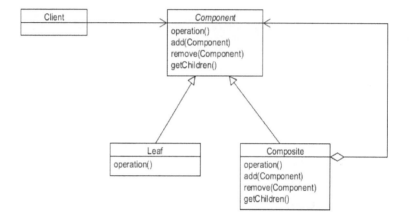

```java
package com.dev.dp.structural.composite;
/**
 First we will create component interface.
 It represents object in composition .
 It has all common operation that will be applicable to both manager and developer.
 */

/**
 * Manager(Composite)
 * Developer(Leaf)
 * Employee(Component)
 */
public interface Employee {

    public void add(Employee emp);
    public void remove(Employee emp);
    public Employee getChild(int i);
    public String getName();
    public double getSalary();
    public void print();
}
```

```java
/** Now we will create manager(composite class).
 * Key point here is that all common method delegates its operations to child objects.
 * It has method to access and modify its children.
 */
import java.util.ArrayList;

public class Manager implements Employee {

    private String name;
    private double salary;

    public Manager(String name, double salary) {
        this.name = name;
        this.salary = salary;
    }

    List<Employee> employees = new ArrayList<Employee>();

    @Override
    public void add(Employee emp) {
        employees.add(emp);
    }

    @Override
    public void remove(Employee emp) {
        employees.remove(emp);
    }

    @Override
    public Employee getChild(int i) {
        return employees.get(i);
    }
```

```java
    @Override
    public String getName() {
        return name;
    }

    @Override
    public double getSalary() {
        return salary;
    }

    @Override
    public void print() {
        System.out.println("-------------");
        System.out.println("Name =" + getName());
        System.out.println("Salary =" + getSalary());
        System.out.println("-------------");

        Iterator<Employee> empIterator = employees.iterator();
        while(empIterator.hasNext()){
            Employee emp= empIterator.next();
            emp.print();
        }
    }

}
```

```java
/**
 * In this class,there are many methods which are not applicable to developer because
 * it is a leaf node.
 */

public class Developer implements Employee {

    private String name;
    private double salary;

    public Developer(String name,double salary){
        this.name = name;
        this.salary = salary;
    }

    @Override
    public void add(Employee emp) {
        // this is leaf node so this method is not applicable to this class.

    }

    @Override
    public void remove(Employee emp) {
        // this is leaf node so this method is not applicable to this class.

    }

    @Override
    public Employee getChild(int i) {
        // this is leaf node so this method is not applicable to this class.
        return null;
    }

    @Override
    public String getName() {
        return name;
    }

    @Override
    public double getSalary() {
        return salary;
    }

    @Override
    public void print() {
        System.out.println("-------------");
        System.out.println("Name ="+getName());
        System.out.println("Salary ="+getSalary());
        System.out.println("-------------");
    }

}
```

```java
package com.dev.dp.structural.composite;

public class CompositePatternTest {

    public static void main(String[] args) {

        Employee emp1 = new Developer("John", 10000);
        Employee emp2 = new Developer("David", 15000);
        Employee manager1 = new Manager("Daniel", 25000);
        manager1.add(emp1);
        manager1.add(emp2);
        Employee emp3 = new Developer("Michael", 20000);
        Manager generalManager = new Manager("Mark", 50000);
        generalManager.add(emp3);
        generalManager.add(manager1);
        generalManager.print();

    }

}
```

Output:

```
|--------------
Name =Mark
Salary =50000.0
--------------

--------------
Name =Michael
Salary =20000.0
--------------

--------------
Name =Daniel
Salary =25000.0
--------------

--------------
Name =John
Salary =10000.0
--------------

--------------
Name =David
Salary =15000.0
--------------
```

When to use Composite Pattern:
 * When you want to represent part-whole hierarchies of objects.
 * When you want clients to be able to ignore the difference between compositions of objects and individual objects. Clients will treat all objects in the composite structure uniformly.

Usage in JDK:
java.awt.Container#add (Component) is a great example of Composite pattern in java and used a lot in Swing.

PROXY PATTERN

The Proxy Pattern provides a surrogate or placeholder for another object to control access to it.

The Proxy Pattern is used to create a representative object that controls access to another object, which may be remote, expensive to create or in need of being secured. One reason for controlling access to an object is to defer the full cost of its creation and initialization until we actually need to use it. Another reason could be to act as a local representative for an object that lives in a different JVM. The Proxy can be very useful in controlling the access to the original object, especially when objects should have different access rights.

In the Proxy Pattern, a client does not directly talk to the original object, it delegates it calls to the proxy object which calls the methods of the original object. The important point is that the client does not know about the proxy, the proxy acts as an original object for the client. But there are many variations to this approach which we will see soon. There are three main variations to the Proxy Pattern:

   * A remote proxy provides a local representative for an object in a different address space.

   * A virtual proxy creates expensive objects on demand.

* A protection proxy controls access to the original object. Protection proxies are useful when objects should have different access rights.

```java
public interface IFolder {

    public void performOperations();
}
```

```java
public class Folder implements IFolder {

    @Override
    public void performOperations() {

        // access folder and perform various operations like copy or cut files
        System.out.println("Performing operation on folder");

    }

}
```

```java
public class User {

    String userName;
    String password;


    public User(String userName, String password) {
        super();
        this.userName = userName;
        this.password = password;
    }

    public String getUserName() {
        return userName;
    }
    public void setUserName(String userName) {
        this.userName = userName;
    }
    public String getPassword() {
        return password;
    }
    public void setPassword(String password) {
        this.password = password;
    }
}
```

```java
public class FolderProxy implements IFolder {

    Folder folder;
    User user;

    public FolderProxy(User user){
        this.user=user;
    }

    @Override
    public void performOperations() {
        if (user.getUserName().equalsIgnoreCase("dev")
                && user.getPassword().equalsIgnoreCase("dev")) {
            folder = new Folder();
            folder.performOperations();
        } else {
            System.out.println("You don't have access to this folder");
        }
    }

}
```

```java
package com.dev.dp.structural.proxy;

public class ProxyPatternTest {

    public static void main(String[] args) {

        User user = new User("dev", "dev");
        FolderProxy folderProxy = new FolderProxy(user);
        System.out.println("When userName and password are correct:");
        folderProxy.performOperations();
        System.out.println("*************************************");
        // if we give wrong userName and Password
        User userWrong = new User("abc", "abc");
        FolderProxy folderProxyWrong = new FolderProxy(userWrong);
        System.out.println("When userName and password are incorrect:");
        folderProxyWrong.performOperations();

    }

}
```

Output:

```
When userName and password are correct:
Performing operation on folder
*************************************
When userName and password are incorrect:
You don't have access to this folder
```

When to use the Proxy Pattern:

Proxy is applicable whenever there is a need for a more versatile or sophisticated reference to an object than a simple pointer. Here are several common situations in which the Proxy pattern is applicable:
* A remote proxy provides a local representative for an object in a different address space.
* A virtual proxy creates expensive objects on demand.
* A protection proxy controls access to the original object. Protection proxies are useful when objects should have different access rights.

Proxy Pattern in JDK:

The following cases are examples of usage of the Proxy Pattern in the JDK.
* java.lang.reflect.Proxy
* java.rmi.* (whole package)

FAÇADE PATTERN

The facade pattern is a structural design pattern. In the facade pattern, a facade classes is used to provide a single interface to set of classes. The facade simplifies a client's interaction with a complex system by localizing the interactions into a single interface. As a result, the client can interact with a single object rather than being required to interact directly in complicated ways with the objects that make up the subsystem.

According to GoF Facade design pattern is: *Provide a unified interface to a set of interfaces in a subsystem. Facade Pattern defines a higher-level interface that makes the subsystem easier to use.*

The Facade does not encapsulate the subsystem classes or interfaces; it just provides a simplified interface to their functionality. A client can access these classes directly. It still exposes the full functionality of the system for the clients who may need it. It just provides a layer to the complex interfaces of the sub-system which makes it easier to use.

Facade design pattern is one among the other design patterns that promote loose coupling. It emphasizes one more important aspect of design which is abstraction. By hiding the complexity behind it and exposing a simple interface it achieves abstraction.

Facade can wrap multiple classes, but a facade is used to an interface to simplify the use of the complex interface, whereas, an adapter is used to convert the interface to an interface the client expects.

Mediator design pattern may look very similar to facade design pattern in terms of abstraction. Mediator abstracts the functionality of the subsystems in this way it is similar to the facade pattern. In the implementation of mediator pattern, subsystem or peers components are aware of the mediator and that interact with it. In the case of facade pattern, subsystems are not aware of the existence of facade. Only facade talks to the subsystems.

```
package com.dev.dp.structural.facade;

public class Class1 {

//Class1's doSomethingComplicated() method takes an integer and returns its cube.
    public int doSomethingComplicated(int x) {
        return x * x * x;
    }
}


package com.dev.dp.structural.facade;

public class Class2 {

//Class2's doAnotherThing() method doubles the cube of an integer and returns it.
    public int doAnotherThing(Class1 class1, int x) {
        return 2 * class1.doSomethingComplicated(x);
    }
}
```

```java
package com.dev.dp.structural.facade;

public class Class3 {

//Class3's doMoreStuff() takes a Class1 object, a Class2 object,and multiply them.
    public int doMoreStuff(Class1 class1, Class2 class2, int x) {
        return class1.doSomethingComplicated(x) * class2.doAnotherThing(class1, x);
    }
}
```

```java
package com.dev.dp.structural.facade;

public class Facade {
//we need to be able to simplify interaction with this system of classes
//so that clients can interact with these classes in a simple, standardized manner.
//We do this with the Facade class.
//The names of these methods clearly indicate what they do,
//and these methods hide the interactions of Class1, Class2, and Class3 from client

    public int cubeX(int x) {
        Class1 class1 = new Class1();
        return class1.doSomethingComplicated(x);
    }

    public int cubeXTimes2(int x) {
        Class1 class1 = new Class1();
        Class2 class2 = new Class2();
        return class2.doAnotherThing(class1, x);
    }

    public int multiplyBoth(int x) {
        Class1 class1 = new Class1();
        Class2 class2 = new Class2();
        Class3 class3 = new Class3();
        return class3.doMoreStuff(class1, class2, x);
    }
}
```

```
package com.dev.dp.structural.facade;

public class FacadePatternTest {

    public static void main(String[] args) {

    Facade facade = new Facade();

    int x = 3;
    System.out.println("Cube of " + x + ":" + facade.cubeX(3));
    System.out.println("Cube of " + x + " times 2:" + facade.cubeXTimes2(3));
    System.out.println(x + " multiply class1 & class2 :" + facade.multiplyBoth(3));
    }

}
```

Output:

```
Cube of 3:27
Cube of 3 times 2:54
3 multiply class1 & class2 :1458
```

Important Points:

* Facade pattern is more like a helper for client applications; it doesn't hide subsystem interfaces from the client. Whether to use Facade or not is completely dependent on client code.

* Facade pattern can be applied at any point of development, usually when the number of interfaces grows and system gets complex.

* Subsystem interfaces are not aware of Facade and they shouldn't have any reference of the Facade interface.

* Facade pattern should be applied for similar kind of interfaces; its purpose is to provide a single interface rather than multiple interfaces that does the similar kind of jobs.

* Subsystem may be dependent with one another. In such case, facade can act as a coordinator and decouple the dependencies between the subsystems.
* We can use factory design pattern with Facade to provide better interface to client systems.

Usage in Java:

In javax.faces.context, **ExternalContext** internally uses ServletContext, HttpSession, HttpServletRequest, HttpServletResponse, etc. It allows the Faces API to be unaware of the nature of its containing application environment.

BRIDGE PATTERN

When we have interface hierarchies in both interfaces as well as implementations, then **builder design pattern** is used to decouple the interfaces from implementation and hiding the implementation details from the client programs.

According to GoF bridge design pattern is: *Decouple an abstraction from its implementation so that the two can vary independently.*

In the bridge pattern, we separate an abstraction and its implementation and develop separate inheritance structures for both the abstraction and the implementer. The abstraction is an interface or abstract class, and the implementer is likewise an interface or abstract class. The abstraction contains a reference to the implementer. Children of the abstraction are referred to as refined abstractions, and children of the implementer are concrete implementers. Since we can change the reference to the implementer in the abstraction, we are able to change the abstraction's implementer at run-time. Changes to the implementer do not affect client code.

The Bridge Pattern's intent is to decouple an abstraction from its implementation so that the two can vary independently. It puts the abstraction and implementation into two different class hierarchies so that both can be extend independently.

BEFORE BRIDGE DESIGN PATTERN

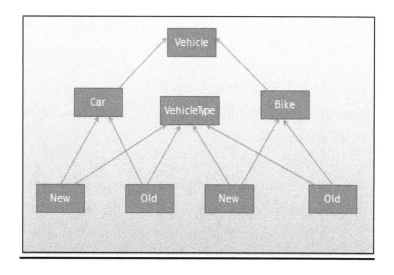

AFTER BRIDGE DESIGN PATTERN

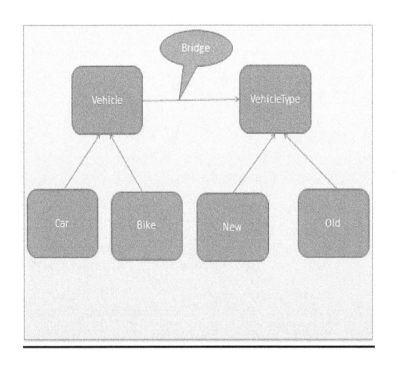

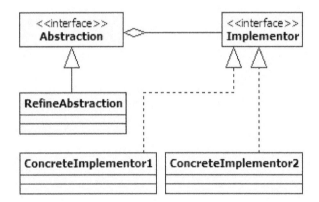

The adapter design pattern helps in making two incompatible classes to work together. But, bridge design pattern decouples the abstraction and implementation by creating two different hierarchies.

```java
package com.dev.dp.structural.bridge;

/**
 * abstraction in bridge pattern
 */
public abstract class Vehicle {
    protected VehicleType type1;
    protected VehicleType type2;

    public Vehicle(VehicleType type1, VehicleType type2) {
        this.type1 = type1;
        this.type2 = type2;
    }

    abstract public void purchase();
}
```

```java
package com.dev.dp.structural.bridge;

/**
 * Implementor for bridge pattern
 */
public interface VehicleType {

    abstract public void book();
}
```

```java
package com.dev.dp.structural.bridge;

/**
 * Refine abstraction 1 in bridge pattern
 */
public class Car extends Vehicle {

    public Car(VehicleType type1, VehicleType type2) {
        super(type1, type2);
    }

    @Override
    public void purchase() {
        System.out.print("Car");
        type1.book();
        type2.book();
    }

}
```

```java
package com.dev.dp.structural.bridge;

/**
 * Refine abstraction 2 in bridge pattern
 */
public class Bike extends Vehicle {

    public Bike(VehicleType type1, VehicleType type2) {
        super(type1, type2);
    }

    @Override
    public void purchase() {
        System.out.print("Bike");
        type1.book();
        type2.book();
    }

}
```

```java
package com.dev.dp.structural.bridge;

/**
 * Concrete implementation 1 for bridge pattern
 * */
public class NewVehicle implements VehicleType {

    @Override
    public void book() {
        System.out.print(" New Vehicle");
    }

}
```

```java
package com.dev.dp.structural.bridge;

/**
 * Concrete implementation 2 for bridge pattern
 * */
public class OldVehicle implements VehicleType {

    @Override
    public void book() {

        System.out.println(" Old Vehicle");
    }

}
```

```java
package com.dev.dp.structural.bridge;

public class BridgePatternTest {

    public static void main(String[] args) {

        Vehicle vehicle1= new Car(new NewVehicle(),new OldVehicle());
        vehicle1.purchase();

        Bike vehicle2 = new Bike(new NewVehicle(),new OldVehicle());
        vehicle2.purchase();
    }

}
```

Output:

```
Car New Vehicle Old Vehicle
Bike New Vehicle Old Vehicle
```

Summary of Bridge Design Pattern:

* Creates two different hierarchies. One for abstraction and another for implementation.

* Avoids permanent binding by removing the dependency between abstraction and implementation.

* We create a bridge that coordinates between abstraction and implementation.

* Abstraction and implementation can be extended separately.

* Should be used when we have needed to switch implementation at runtime.

* Client should not be impacted if there is modification in implementation of abstraction.

* Best used when you have multiple implementations.

Usage in JDK:

* AWT (It provides an abstraction layer which maps onto the native OS the windowing support.)

* JDBC

DECORATOR PATTERN

The intent of the Decorator Design Pattern is to attach additional responsibilities to an object dynamically. Decorators provide a flexible alternative to sub-classing for extending functionality.

The Decorator Pattern is used to extend the functionality of an object dynamically without having to change the original class source or using inheritance. This is accomplished by creating an object wrapper referred to as a Decorator around the actual object.

The Decorator object is designed to have the same interface as the underlying object. This allows a client object to interact with the Decorator object in exactly the same manner as it would with the underlying actual object. The Decorator object contains a reference to the actual object. The Decorator object receives all requests (calls) from a client. In turn, it forwards these calls to the underlying object. The Decorator object adds some additional functionality before or after forwarding requests to the underlying object. This ensures that the additional functionality can be added to a given object externally at runtime without modifying its structure.

We use inheritance or composition to extend the behavior of an object but this is done at compile time and it's applicable to all the instances of the class. We can't add any new functionality of remove any existing behavior at runtime – this is when Decorator pattern comes into picture.

Component Interface – The interface or abstract class defining the methods that will be implemented. In our case Icecream will be the component interface.

```
package com.dev.dp.structural.decorator;

public interface Icecream {

    public String makeIcecream();
}
```

Component Implementation – The basic implementation of the component interface. We can have SimpleIcecream class as our component implementation.

```
package com.dev.dp.structural.decorator;

public class SimpleIcecream implements Icecream {

    @Override
    public String makeIcecream() {

        return "Base-Icecream ";
    }

}
```

Decorator – Decorator class implements the component interface and it has a HAS-A relationship with the component interface. The component variable should be accessible to the child decorator classes, so we will make this variable protected.

```
package com.dev.dp.structural.decorator;

public class IcecreamDecorator implements Icecream {

    protected Icecream specialIcecream;

    public IcecreamDecorator(Icecream specialIcecream){
        this.specialIcecream = specialIcecream;
    }

    @Override
    public String makeIcecream() {
        return specialIcecream.makeIcecream();
    }

}
```

Concrete Decorators – Extending the base decorator functionality and modifying the component behavior

accordingly. We can have concrete decorator classes
as NuttyIcecreamDecorator & HoneyIcecreamDecorator.

```java
package com.dev.dp.structural.decorator;

public class NuttyDecorator extends IcecreamDecorator {

    public NuttyDecorator(Icecream specialIcecream) {
        super(specialIcecream);
    }

    public String makeIcecream(){
        return specialIcecream.makeIcecream() + addNuts();
    }

    private String addNuts() {
        return "+ Crunchy Nuts ";
    }
}
```

```java
package com.dev.dp.structural.decorator;

public class HoneyDecorator extends IcecreamDecorator {

    public HoneyDecorator(Icecream specialIcecream) {
        super(specialIcecream);
    }

    public String makeIcecream(){
        return specialIcecream.makeIcecream() + addHoney();
    }

    private String addHoney() {
        return "+ Sweet Honey ";
    }
}
```

```
package com.dev.dp.structural.decorator;

public class DecoratorPatternTest {

  public static void main(String[] args) {

    Icecream icecream = new HoneyDecorator(new NuttyDecorator(new SimpleIcecream()));
    System.out.println(icecream.makeIcecream());
  }

}
```

Output:

Base-Icecream + Crunchy Nuts + Sweet Honey

When to use the Decorator Design Pattern:

Use the Decorator pattern in the following cases:
* To add responsibilities to individual objects dynamically and transparently, that is, without affecting other objects.

* For responsibilities that can be withdrawn.

* When extension by sub-classing is impractical. Sometimes a large number of independent extensions are possible and would produce an explosion of subclasses to support every combination. Or a class definition may be hidden or otherwise unavailable for sub-classing.

* It's easy to maintain and extend when the number of choices are more.

Usage in Java:

* Decorator pattern is used a lot in Java IO classes, such as FileReader, BufferedReader etc.

The disadvantage of decorator pattern is that it uses a lot of similar kind of objects (decorators).

FLYWEIGHT PATTERN

In the flyweight pattern, instead of creating large numbers of similar objects, objects are reused. This can be used to reduce memory requirements and instantiation time and related costs.

Flyweight design pattern is used when we need to create a lot of Objects of a class. Since every object consumes memory space that can be crucial for low memory devices, such as mobile devices or embedded systems, flyweight design pattern can be applied to reduce the load on memory by sharing objects.
Before we apply flyweight design pattern, we need to consider following factors:

> * The number of Objects to be created by application should be huge.
> * The object creation is heavy on memory and it can be time consuming too.

Sometimes too many objects can slow things down. Too many objects might consume a large piece of memory and can slow down the application or even cause out of memory problems. As a good programmer, one should keep track of instantiated objects and control the object creation in an application. This is especially true, when we have a lot of similar objects and two objects from the pool don't have many differences between them.
Sometimes the objects in an application might have great similarities and be of a similar kind (a similar kind here means that most of their properties have similar values and only a few of them vary in value). In case they are also heavy objects to create, they should be controlled by the application developer. Otherwise, they might consume

much of the memory and eventually slow down the whole application.

The Flyweight Pattern is designed to control such kind of object creation and provides you with a basic caching mechanism. It allows you to create one object per type (the type here differs by a property of that object), and if you ask for an object with the same property (already created), it will return you the same object instead of creating a new one.

Flyweight Pattern Example in JDK:

All the wrapper classes valueOf () method uses cached objects showing use of Flyweight design pattern. The best example is Java String class String Pool implementation.

TEMPLATE METHOD PATTERN

The Template Pattern defines the skeleton of an algorithm in an operation, deferring some steps to subclasses. Template Method lets subclasses to redefine certain steps of an algorithm without changing the algorithm's structure.

The Template Method pattern can be used in situations when there is an algorithm, some steps of which could be implemented in multiple different ways. In such scenarios, the Template Method pattern suggests keeping the outline of the algorithm in a separate method referred to as a template method inside a class, which may be referred to as a template class, leaving out the specific implementations of the variant portions (steps that can be implemented in multiple different ways) of the algorithm to different subclasses of this class.

The Template class does not necessarily have to leave the implementation to subclasses in its entirety. Instead, as part of providing the outline of the algorithm, the Template class can also provide some amount of implementation that can be considered as invariant across different implementations. It can even provide default implementation for the variant parts, if appropriate. Only specific details will be implemented inside different subclasses. This type of implementation eliminates the need for duplicate code, which means a minimum amount of code to be written.

* Template method should consist of certain steps whose order is fixed and for some of the methods; implementation differs from base class to subclass. Template method should be final.

* Most of the times, subclasses calls methods from super class but in template pattern, superclass template method

calls methods from subclasses, this is known as Hollywood Principle – *"don't call us, we'll call you."*

* Methods in base class with default implementation are referred as **Hooks** and they are intended to be overridden by subclasses, if you want some of the methods to be not overridden, you can make them final, for example in our case we can make doPack () method final because if we don't want subclasses to override it.

```java
public abstract class PurchaseOrderTemplate {

    public abstract void doSelect();
    public abstract void doPayment();
    public final void doPack(){
        System.out.println("Gift wrap done.");
    }
    public abstract void doDelivery();
    public final void processOrder(){
        doSelect();
        doPayment();
        doPack();
        doDelivery();
    }
}
```

```java
package com.dev.dp.behavioral.templateMethod;

public class StorePurchaseOrder extends PurchaseOrderTemplate {

    @Override
    public void doSelect() {
        System.out.println("Customer chooses the item from shelf.");
    }

    @Override
    public void doPayment() {
        System.out.println("Pays at counter through cash/POS");
    }

    @Override
    public void doDelivery() {
        System.out.println("Item deliverd to in delivery counter.");
    }

}
```

```java
package com.dev.dp.behavioral.templateMethod;

public class OnlinePurchaseOrder extends PurchaseOrderTemplate {

    @Override
    public void doSelect() {
        System.out.println("Item added to online shopping cart,");
        System.out.println("Get gift wrap preference,");
        System.out.println("Get delivery address.");
    }

    @Override
    public void doPayment() {
        System.out.println("Online Payment through Netbanking/Cards.");
    }

    @Override
    public void doDelivery() {
        System.out.println("Ship the item through post to delivery address");
    }

}
```

```
package com.dev.dp.behavioral.templateMethod;

public class TemplateMethodPatternTest {

    public static void main(String[] args) {
        PurchaseOrderTemplate online= new OnlinePurchaseOrder();
        online.processOrder();
        PurchaseOrderTemplate offline= new StorePurchaseOrder();
        offline.processOrder();|
    }

}
```

Output:

```
Item added to online shopping cart,
Get gift wrap preference,
Get delivery address.
Online Payment through Netbanking/Cards.
Gift wrap done.
Ship the item through post to delivery address
Customer chooses the item from shelf.
Pays at counter through cash/POS
Gift wrap done.
Item deliverd to in delivery counter.
```

When to use the Template Design Pattern:

* To implement the invariant parts of an algorithm once and leave it up to subclasses to implement the behavior that can vary.

* When common behavior among subclasses should be factored and localized in a common class to avoid code duplication. You first identify the differences in the existing

code and then separate the differences into new operations. Finally, you replace the differing code with a template method that calls one of these new operations.

Usage in JDK:

* All non-abstract methods of java.io.InputStream, java.io.OutputStream, java.io.Reader and java.io.Writer. e.g. - java.io.InputStream#skip (), java.io.InputStream#read ()
* All non-abstract methods of java.util.AbstractList, java.util.AbstractSet and java.util.AbstractMap. e.g. – java.util.AbstractList#indexOf (), java.util.Collections#sort ().

MEDIATOR PATTERN

Mediator promotes loose coupling by keeping objects from referring to each other explicitly, and it lets you vary their interaction independently.

Mediator design pattern is used to provide a centralized communication medium between different objects in a system.

Rather than interacting directly with each other, objects ask the Mediator to interact on their behalf which results in reusability and loose coupling. It encapsulates the interaction between the objects and makes them independent from each other. This allows them to vary their interaction with other objects in a totally different way by implementing a different mediator. The Mediator helps to reduce the complexity of the classes. Each object no longer has to know in detail about how to interact with the other objects. The coupling between objects goes from tight and brittle to loose and agile.

Mediator design pattern is very helpful in an enterprise application where multiple objects are interacting with each other. If the objects interact with each other directly, the system components are tightly-coupled with each other that make maintainability cost higher and not flexible to extend easily. Mediator pattern focuses on provide a mediator between objects for communication and help in implementing lose-coupling between objects.

Air traffic controller is a great example of mediator pattern where the airport control room works as a mediator for communication between different flights. Mediator works as a router between objects and it can have its own logic to provide way of communication.

The major participants of the Mediator Pattern are:
* Mediator: Defines an interface for communicating with Colleague objects.
* ConcreteMediator: Implements cooperative behavior by coordinating Colleague objects. It also knows and maintains its colleagues.
* Colleague Classes: Each Colleague class knows its Mediator objects. Each colleague communicates with its mediator whenever it would have otherwise communicated with another colleague.

```java
/**
 Colleague A wants to talk, and Colleague B wants to fight with mediator.
 When they do some action(i.e., doSomething()),
 they invoke mediator to do that.
 */

public interface IMediator {

    public void talk();
    public void fight();
    public void registerA(ColleagueA a);
    public void registerB(ColleagueB b);
}
```

```java
public class ConcreteMediator implements IMediator {

    ColleagueA talk;
    ColleagueB fight;

    @Override
    public void talk() {
        System.out.println("Mediator is talking");
        //let the talk colleague do some stuff
    }

    @Override
    public void fight() {
        System.out.println("Mediator is fighting");
        //let the fight colleague do some stuff
    }

    @Override
    public void registerA(ColleagueA a) {
        this.talk=a;
    }

    @Override
    public void registerB(ColleagueB b) {
        this.fight=b;
    }

}
```

```java
package com.dev.dp.behavioral.mediator;

public abstract class Colleague {
    IMediator mediator;
    public abstract void doSomething();
}
```

```java
package com.dev.dp.behavioral.mediator;

public class ColleagueA extends Colleague {

    public ColleagueA(IMediator mediator){
        this.mediator= mediator;
        this.mediator.registerA(this);
    }

    @Override
    public void doSomething() {
        this.mediator.talk();
    }

}
```

```java
package com.dev.dp.behavioral.mediator;

public class ColleagueB extends Colleague {

    public ColleagueB(IMediator mediator){
        this.mediator=mediator;
        this.mediator.registerB(this);
    }

    @Override
    public void doSomething() {
        this.mediator.fight();
    }

}
```

```
package com.dev.dp.behavioral.mediator;

public class MediatorPatternTest {

    public static void main(String[] args) {
        IMediator mediator = new ConcreteMediator();

        ColleagueA talkColleague = new ColleagueA(mediator);
        talkColleague.doSomething();

        ColleagueB fightColleague = new ColleagueB(mediator);
        fightColleague.doSomething();
    }

}
```

Output:

```
Mediator is talking
Mediator is fighting
```

When to use the Mediator Pattern:

* A set of objects communicate in well-defined but complex ways. The resulting interdependencies are unstructured and difficult to understand.

* Reusing an object is difficult because it refers to and communicates with many other objects.

* A behavior that's distributed between several classes should be customizable without a lot of sub-classing.

Mediator Pattern in JDK:

* java.util.Timer class scheduleXXX () methods.

* java Concurrency Executor execute () method.
* java.lang.reflect.Method invoke () method.

CHAIN OF RESPONSIBILITY

Chain of responsibility pattern is used to achieve **lose coupling** in software design where a request from client is passed to a chain of objects to process them. Then the object in the chain will decide themselves who will be processing the request and whether the request is required to be sent to the next object in the chain or not.

When there is more than one objects that can handle or fulfill a client request, the pattern recommends giving each of these objects a chance to process the request in some sequential order. Applying the pattern in such a case, each of these potential handlers can be arranged in the form of a chain, with each object having a reference to the next object in the chain. The first object in the chain receives the request and decides either to handle the request or to pass it on to the next object in the chain. The request flows through all objects in the chain one after the other until the request is handled by one of the handlers in the chain or the request reaches the end of the chain without getting processed.

Let's see the example of chain of responsibility pattern in JDK and then we will proceed to implement a real life example of this pattern. We know that we can have multiple catch blocks in a try-catch block code. Here every catch block is kind of a processor to process that particular exception. So when any exception occurs in the try block its send to the first catch block to process. If the catch block is not able to process it, it forwards the request to next object in chain i.e. next catch block. If even the last catch block is not able to process it, the exception is thrown outside of the chain to the calling program.

Other examples are ATM money dispenser, Servlet Filter and finally java's own Exception Handling mechanism. We know exception handling better than anybody else and we are daily living with it. This qualifies as the best example for chain of responsibility.

In ATM Dispense machine, the user enters the amount to be dispensed and the machine dispense amount in terms of defined currency bills such as 50$, 20$, 10$ etc. If the user enters an amount that is not multiples of 10, it throws error.

```java
//This class is the request object.
public class Number {

    private int number;

    public int getNumber() {
        return number;
    }

    public Number(int num){
        number=num;
    }

}
```

```java
//This is the interface that acts as a chain link.
public interface Chain {
    public void setNext(Chain nextInChain);
    public void process(Number request);
}
```

```java
package com.dev.dp.behavioral.chainOfResponsibility;

public class PositiveNumberProcessor implements Chain {

    private Chain nextInChain;

    @Override
    public void setNext(Chain c) {
        nextInChain = c;
    }

    @Override
    public void process(Number request) {

        if (request.getNumber() > 0) {
            System.out.println("PositiveNumberProcessor : " + request.getNumber());
        } else {
            nextInChain.process(request);
        }
    }
}
```

```java
package com.dev.dp.behavioral.chainOfResponsibility;

public class NegativeNumberProcessor implements Chain {

    private Chain nextInChain;

    @Override
    public void setNext(Chain c) {
        nextInChain=c;
    }

    @Override
    public void process(Number request) {

        if (request.getNumber() < 0) {
            System.out.println("NegativeNumberProcessor : " + request.getNumber());
        } else {
            nextInChain.process(request);
        }
    }
}
```

```
package com.dev.dp.behavioral.chainOfResponsibility;

public class ZeroProcessor implements Chain {

    private Chain nextInChain;

    @Override
    public void setNext(Chain c) {
        nextInChain = c;
    }

    @Override
    public void process(Number request) {

        if (request.getNumber() == 0) {
            System.out.println("ZeroProcessor : " + request.getNumber());
        } else {
            nextInChain.process(request);
        }
    }
}
```

```
package com.dev.dp.behavioral.chainOfResponsibility;

public class CORPatternTest {

    public static void main(String[] args) {

        //configure Chain of Responsibility
        Chain c1 = new NegativeNumberProcessor();
        Chain c2 = new ZeroProcessor();
        Chain c3 = new PositiveNumberProcessor();
        c1.setNext(c2);
        c2.setNext(c3);

        //calling chain of responsibility
        c1.process(new Number(99));
        c1.process(new Number(-30));
        c1.process(new Number(0));
        c1.process(new Number(100));

    }
}
```

Output:

```
PositiveNumberProcessor : 99
NegativeNumberProcessor : -30
ZeroProcessor : 0
PositiveNumberProcessor : 100
```

When to use the Chain of Responsibility Pattern:

Use Chain of Responsibility when
* More than one object may handle a request, and the handler isn't known a priori. The handler should be ascertained automatically.

* You want to issue a request to one of several objects without specifying the receiver explicitly.

* The set of objects that can handle a request should be specified dynamically.

Chain of Responsibility Pattern Examples in JDK:

* java.util.logging.Logger#log ()
* javax.servlet.Filter#doFilter ()

OBSERVER PATTERN

In observer design pattern multiple observer objects registers with a subject for change notification. When the state of subject changes, it notifies the observers. Objects that listen or watch for change are called observers and the object that is being watched for is called subject.

Pattern involved is also called as publish-subscribe pattern.

* Subject provides interface for observers to register and unregister themselves with the subject.

* Subject knows who its subscribers are.

* Multiple observers can subscribe for notifications.

* Subject publishes the notifications.

* Subject just sends the notification saying the state has changed. It does not pass any state information.

* Once the notification is received from subject, observers call the subject and get data that is changed.

The above last two points are not strictly followed in observer design pattern implementation. Along with the notification, state is also passed in some implementation so that the observer need not query back to know the status. It is better not to do this way.

There are four participants in the Observer pattern:

* **Subject,** which is used to register observers. Objects use this interface to register as observers and also to remove themselves from being observers.

* **Observer** defines an updating interface for objects that should be notified of changes in a subject. All observers need to implement the Observer interface. This interface has a method update (), which gets called when the Subject's state changes.

* **ConcreteSubject,** stores the state of interest to ConcreteObserver objects. It sends a notification to its observers when its state changes. A concrete subject always implements the Subject interface. The notifyObservers () method is used to update all the current observers whenever the state changes.

* **ConcreateObserver** maintains a reference to a ConcreteSubject object and implements the Observer interface. Each observer registers with a concrete subject to receive updates.

Java provides inbuilt platform for implementing Observer pattern through *java.util.Observable* class and *java.util.Observer* interface. However it's not widely used because the implementation is really simple and most of the times we don't want to end up extending a class just for implementing Observer pattern as java doesn't provide multiple inheritances in classes.

Let us take a blog and subscriber example for observer design pattern sample implementation. Assume that there is a blog and users register to that blog for update. When a new article is posted in the blog, it will send update to the registered users saying a new article is posted. Then the user will access the blog and read the new article posted. In this example, blog is the subject and user is the observer.

```java
package com.dev.dp.behavioral.observer;

public interface Subject {

    public void registerObserver(Observer observer);
    public void notifyObserver();
    public void unregisterObserver(Observer observer);
    public Object getUpdate();
}
```

```java
package com.dev.dp.behavioral.observer;

public interface Observer {

    public void update();
    public void setSubject(Subject sub);
}
```

```
//ConcreteSubject
    @Override
    public Object getUpdate() {
        Object changedState = null;
        // should have logic to send the
        // state change to querying observer
        if (stateChange) {
            changedState = "Observer Design Pattern";
        }
        return changedState;
    }

    public void postNewArticle() {
        stateChange = true;
        notifyObserver();
    }
}
```

```
//Concrete Observer
public class User implements Observer {

    private String article;
    private Subject blog;
    @Override
    public void update() {
        System.out.println("State change reported by Subject.");
        article = (String) blog.getUpdate();
    }

    @Override
    public void setSubject(Subject blog) {
        this.blog = blog;
        article = "No New Article!";
    }

    public String getArticle() {
        return article;
    }

}
```

```
package com.dev.dp.behavioral.observer;

public class ObserverPatternTest {

    public static void main(String[] args) {
        Blog blog = new Blog();
        User user1 = new User();
        User user2 = new User();
        blog.registerObserver(user1);
        blog.registerObserver(user2);
        user1.setSubject(blog);
        user2.setSubject(blog);
        System.out.println(user1.getArticle());
        blog.postNewArticle();
        System.out.println(user1.getArticle());
    }
}
```

Output:

```
No New Article!
State change reported by Subject.
Observer notified !
State change reported by Subject.
Observer notified !
Observer Design Pattern
```

When to use the Observer Pattern:

Use the Observer pattern in any of the following situations:
* When an abstraction has two aspects, one dependent on the other. Encapsulating these aspects in separate objects lets you vary and reuse them independently.

* When a change to one object requires changing others, and you don't know how many objects need to be changed?

* When an object should be able to notify other objects without making assumptions about who these objects are. In other words, you don't want these objects tightly coupled.

Usage in Java:

* java.util.EventListener in Swing

* javax.servlet.http.HttpSessionBindingListener

* javax.servlet.http.HttpSessionAttributeListener

STRATEGY PATTERN

The Strategy pattern is useful when there is a set of related algorithms and a client object needs to be able to dynamically pick and choose an algorithm from this set that suits its current need. The Strategy pattern suggests keeping the implementation of each of the algorithms in a separate class. Each such algorithm encapsulated in a separate class is referred to as a strategy. An object that uses a Strategy object is often referred to as a context object.

In other words, Strategy pattern is used when we have multiple algorithms for a specific task and client decides the actual implementation to be used at runtime. Strategy pattern is also known as **Policy Pattern**. We define multiple algorithms and let client application pass the algorithm to be used as a parameter. One of the best example of this pattern is Collections.sort () method that takes Comparator parameter. Based on the different implementations of Comparator interfaces, the Objects are getting sorted in different ways.

The strategy pattern is one way that composition can be used as an alternative to sub-classing. Rather than providing different behaviors via subclasses overriding methods in super classes, the strategy pattern allows different behaviors to be placed in Concrete Strategy classes which share the common Strategy interface. A Context object contains a reference to a Strategy. By changing the Context's Strategy, different behaviors can be obtained.

```java
public interface Strategy {

    public void sort(int [] numbers);
}
```

```java
package com.dev.dp.behavioral.strategy;

public class Context {

    private Strategy strategy ;

    public Context(Strategy strategy){
        this.strategy=strategy;
    }

    public void arrange(int [] input){
        strategy.sort(input);
    }
}
```

```java
public class BubbleSort implements Strategy {

    @Override
    public void sort(int[] numbers) {
        System.out.println("sorting array using bubble sort strategy");
    }
}
```

```java
public class InsertionSort implements Strategy {

    @Override
    public void sort(int[] numbers) {
        System.out.println("sorting array using insertion sort strategy");
    }

}
```

```java
public class MergeSort implements Strategy {

    @Override
    public void sort(int[] numbers) {
        System.out.println("sorting array using merge sort strategy");
    }

}
```

```java
public class QuickSort implements Strategy {

    @Override
    public void sort(int[] numbers) {
        System.out.println("sorting array using quick sort strategy");
    }
}
```

```java
package com.dev.dp.behavioral.strategy;

public class StrategyPatternTest {

    public static void main(String[] args) {

        int[] var = {1, 2, 3, 4, 5 };

        //We can provide any strategy to do the sorting
        Context ctx = new Context(new BubbleSort());
        ctx.arrange(var);

        // we can change the strategy without changing Context class
        ctx = new Context(new QuickSort());
        ctx.arrange(var);

    }
}
```

Output:

```
sorting array using bubble sort strategy
sorting array using quick sort strategy
```

When to use the Strategy Design Pattern

Use the Strategy pattern when:

* Many related classes differ only in their behavior. Strategies provide a way to configure a class with one of many behaviors.

* You need different variants of an algorithm. For example, you might define algorithms reflecting different space/time trade-offs. Strategies can be used when these variants are implemented as a class hierarchy of algorithms.

* An algorithm uses data that clients shouldn't know about. Use the Strategy pattern to avoid exposing complex, algorithm-specific data structures.

* A class defines many behaviors, and these appear as multiple conditional statements in its operations. Instead of many conditionals, move related conditional branches into their own Strategy class.

Strategy Pattern in JDK:
   * java.util.Comparator#compare ()
   * javax.servlet.http.HttpServlet
   * javax.servlet.Filter#doFilter ()

COMMAND PATTERN

The command pattern is a behavioral object design pattern. In the command pattern, a Command interface declares a method for executing a particular action. Concrete Command classes implement the execute () method of the Command interface, and this execute () method invokes the appropriate action method of a Receiver class that the

Concrete Command class contains. The Receiver class performs a particular action. A Client class is responsible for creating a Concrete Command and setting the Receiver of the Concrete Command. An Invoker class contains a reference to a Command and has a method to execute the Command.

In the command pattern, the invoker is decoupled from the action performed by the receiver. The invoker has no knowledge of the receiver. The invoker invokes a command, and the command executes the appropriate action of the receiver. Thus, the invoker can invoke commands without knowing the details of the action to be performed. In addition, this decoupling means that changes to the receiver's action don't directly affect the invocation of the action.

The command pattern can be used to perform 'undo' functionality. In this case, the Command interface should include an unexecuted () method.

In other words, it's used to implement **lose coupling** in a request-response model. In command pattern, the request is send to the *invoker* and invoker passes it to the encapsulated *command* object. Command object passes the request to the appropriate method of *Receiver* to perform the specific action. The client program creates the receiver object and then attaches it to the Command. Then it creates the invoker object and attaches the command object to perform an action. Now when client program executes the action, it's processed based on the command and receiver object.

To understand command design pattern we should understand the associated key terms like client, command, command implementation, invoker, and receiver.

* **Command** is an interface with execute method. It is the core of contract.

* A **client** creates an instance of a command implementation and associates it with a receiver.

* An **invoker** instructs the command to perform an action.

* A **Command implementation**'s instance creates a binding between the receiver and an action.

* **Receiver** is the object that knows the actual steps to perform the action. Any class may serve as a Receiver.

```
/**
 Command interface with an execute() method.
 */
public interface Command {

    public void execute();
}
```

```java
/**
 Lunch is a receiver.
*/
public class Lunch {

    public void makeLunch(){
        System.out.println("Lunch is being made");
    }
}
```

```java
/**
 LunchCommand implements Command. It contains a reference to Lunch, a receiver.
 Its execute() method invokes the appropriate action on the receiver.
*/
public class LunchCommand implements Command {

    Lunch lunch;

    public LunchCommand(Lunch lunch) {
        this.lunch = lunch;
    }

    @Override
    public void execute() {
        lunch.makeLunch();
    }
}
```

```java
/**
Dinner is also a receiver.
*/
public class Dinner {
    public void makeDinner(){
        System.out.println("Dinner is being made.");
    }
}
```

```java
/**
The DinnerCommand is similar to LunchCommand.
It contains a reference to Dinner, a receiver.
Its execute() method invokes the makeDinner() action of the Dinner object.
*/
public class DinnerCommand implements Command {

    Dinner dinner;

    public DinnerCommand(Dinner dinner){
        this.dinner=dinner;
    }

    @Override
    public void execute() {
        dinner.makeDinner();
    }
}
```

```java
/**
MealInvoker is the invoker class.
It contains a reference to the Command to invoke.
Its invoke() method calls the execute() method of the Command.
*/
public class MealInvoker {

    Command command;

    public MealInvoker(Command command) {
        this.command = command;
    }

    public void setCommand(Command command) {
        this.command = command;
    }

    public void invoke() {
        command.execute();
    }

}
```

```
package com.dev.dp.behavioral.command;

public class CommandPatternDemo {

    public static void main(String[] args) {

        Lunch lunch = new Lunch(); // receiver
        Command lunchCommand = new LunchCommand(lunch); // concrete command

        Dinner dinner = new Dinner(); // receiver
        Command dinnerCommand = new DinnerCommand(dinner); // concrete command

        MealInvoker mealInvoker = new MealInvoker(lunchCommand); // invoker
        mealInvoker.invoke();

        mealInvoker.setCommand(dinnerCommand);
        mealInvoker.invoke();
    }

}
```

Output:

```
Lunch is being made
Dinner is being made.
```

When to use the Command Design Pattern:

Use the Command pattern when you want to:

* Parameterize objects by an action to perform.

* Support undo. The Command's Execute operation can store state for reversing its effects in the command itself. The Command interface must have an added Un-execute operation that reverses the effects of a previous call to Execute. Executed commands are stored in a history list. Unlimited-level undo and redo is achieved by traversing

this list backwards and forwards calling Un-execute and Execute, respectively.

* Structure a system around high-level operations built on primitives operations. Such a structure is common in information systems that support transactions. The Command pattern offers a way to model transactions. Commands have a common interface, letting you invoke all transactions the same way. The pattern also makes it easy to extend the system with new transactions.

Command Pattern JDK Example:

* Runnable Interface (java.lang.Runnable) and Swing Action (javax.swing.Action) uses command pattern.

VISITOR PATTERN

Visitor pattern is used when we have to perform an operation on a group of similar kind of Objects. With the help of visitor pattern, we can move the operational logic from the objects to another class. For example, think of a Shopping cart where we can add different type of items (Elements), when we click on checkout button, it calculates the total amount to be paid. Now we can have the calculation logic in item classes or we can move out this logic to another class using visitor pattern. So using visitor pattern we can move out logics to another class.

The Visitor pattern allows the operation to be defined without changing the class of any of the objects in the collection. To accomplish this, the Visitor pattern suggests defining the operation in a separate class referred to as a visitor class. This separates the operation from the object collection that it operates on. For every new operation to be defined, a new visitor class is created. Since the operation is to be performed across a set of objects, the visitor needs a way of accessing the public members of these objects.

Following components are involved in visitor pattern.

Visitor: Declares a Visit operation for each class of ConcreteElement in the object structure. The operation's name and signature identifies the class that sends the Visit request to the visitor. That lets the visitor determine the concrete class of the element being visited. Then the visitor can access the element directly through its particular interface.

ConcreteVisitor: Implements each operation declared by Visitor. Each operation implements a fragment of the algorithm defined for the corresponding class of object in the structure. ConcreteVisitor provides the context for the algorithm and stores its local state. This state often accumulates results during the traversal of the structure.

Element: Defines an Accept operation that takes a visitor as an argument.

ConcreteElement: Implements an Accept operation that takes a visitor as an argument.

ObjectStructure:

   * Can enumerate its elements.

   * May provide a high-level interface to allow the visitor to visit its elements.

   * May either be a composite or a collection such as a list or a set.

To implement visitor pattern, first of all we will create different type of items (Elements) to be used in shopping cart.

```
public interface ShoppingCartElement {
//Notice that accept method takes Visitor argument,
//we can have some other methods also specific for items but for simplicity
//I am not going into that much detail and focusing on visitor pattern only.
    public int accept(ShoppingCartVisitor visitor);
}
```

Let's create some concrete classes for different types of
item.

```
package com.dev.dp.behavioral.visitor;

public class Book implements ShoppingCartElement {

    private int price;
    private String isbnNumber;

    public Book(int cost, String isbn){
        this.price=cost;
        this.isbnNumber=isbn;
    }

    public int getPrice() {
        return price;
    }

    public String getIsbnNumber() {
        return isbnNumber;
    }

    @Override
    //Notice the implementation of accept() method in concrete classes,
    //its calling visit() method of Visitor and passing itself as argument.
    public int accept(ShoppingCartVisitor visitor) {
        // TODO Auto-generated method stub
        return visitor.visit(this);
    }
}
```

```java
package com.dev.dp.behavioral.visitor;

public class Fruit implements ShoppingCartElement {

    private int pricePerKg;
    private int weight;
    private String name;

    public Fruit(int priceKg, int wt, String nm){
        this.pricePerKg=priceKg;
        this.weight=wt;
        this.name = nm;
    }

    public int getPricePerKg() {
        return pricePerKg;
    }

    public int getWeight() {
        return weight;
    }

    public String getName(){
        return this.name;
    }

    @Override
    public int accept(ShoppingCartVisitor visitor) {
        // TODO Auto-generated method stub
        return visitor.visit(this);
    }

}
```

We have visit () method for different type of items in Visitor interface that will be implemented by concrete visitor class.

```
public interface ShoppingCartVisitor {

    //We have visit() method for different type of items in Visitor interface
    //that will be implemented by concrete visitor class.
    int visit(Book book);
    int visit(Fruit fruit);
}
```

Now we will implement visitor interface and every item will have its own logic to calculate the cost.

```
public class ShoppingCartVisitorImpl implements ShoppingCartVisitor {

    @Override
    public int visit(Book book) {
        int cost=0;
        //apply 5$ discount if book price is greater than 50
        if(book.getPrice() > 50){
            cost = book.getPrice()-5;
        }else cost = book.getPrice();
        System.out.println("Book ISBN::"+book.getIsbnNumber() + " cost ="+cost);
        return cost;
    }

    @Override
    public int visit(Fruit fruit) {
        int cost = fruit.getPricePerKg()*fruit.getWeight();
        System.out.println(fruit.getName() + " cost = "+cost);
        return cost;
    }

}
```

Let's see how we can use it in client applications.

```
public class VisitorPatternTest {

    public static void main(String[] args) {

        ShoppingCartElement[] items = new ShoppingCartElement[]{new Book(20, "1234"),
                    new Book(100, "5678"),
                    new Fruit(10, 2, "Banana"), new Fruit(5, 5, "Apple")};

            int total = calculatePrice(items);
            System.out.println("Total Cost = "+total);
    }

    private static int calculatePrice(ShoppingCartElement[] items) {

        ShoppingCartVisitor visitor = new ShoppingCartVisitorImpl();
        int sum=0;
        for(ShoppingCartElement item : items){
            sum = sum + item.accept(visitor);
        }
        return sum;
    }
}
```

Output:

```
Book ISBN::1234 cost =20
Book ISBN::5678 cost =95
Banana cost = 20
Apple cost = 25
Total Cost = 160
```

The benefit of this pattern is that if the logic of operation changes, then we need to make change only in the visitor implementation rather than doing it in all the item classes

When to use the Visitor Design Pattern:

Use the Visitor pattern when:
* An object structure contains many classes of objects with differing interfaces, and you want to perform operations on these objects that depend on their concrete classes.

* Many distinct and unrelated operations need to be performed on objects in an object structure, and you want to avoid "polluting" their classes with these operations.

Visitor lets you keep related operations together by defining them in one class. When the object structure is shared by many applications, use Visitor to put operations in just those applications that need them.

* The classes defining the object structure rarely change, but you often want to define new operations over the structure. Changing the object structure classes requires redefining the interface to all visitors, which is potentially costly. If the object structure classes change often, then it's probably better to define the operations in those classes.

Visitor Design Pattern in JDK:

*

javax.lang.model.element.Element and javax.lang.model.element.ElementVisitor
*

javax.lang.model.type.TypeMirror and javax.lang.model.type.TypeVisitor

STATE PATTERN

State design pattern is used when an Object change its behavior when it's internal state changes

The state of an object can be defined as its exact condition at any given point of time, depending on the values of its properties or attributes. The set of methods implemented by a class constitutes the behavior of its instances. Whenever there is a change in the values of its attributes, we say that the state of an object has changed.

When a Context object is first created, it initializes itself with its initial State object. This State object becomes the current State object for the context. By replacing the current State object with a new State object, the context transitions to a new state. When an application object makes a call to a Context method (behavior), it forwards the method call to its current State object.

Context: Defines the interface of interest to clients.

Maintains an instance of a ConcreteState subclass that defines the current state.

State: Defines an interface for encapsulating the behavior associated with a particular state of the Context.

ConcreteState subclasses: Each subclass implements a behavior associated with a state of the Context.

In the state pattern, we have a Context class, and this class has a State reference to a Concrete State instance. The State interface declares particular methods that represent the behaviors of a particular state. Concrete States implement these behaviors. By changing a Context's Concrete State, we change its behavior. In essence, in the state pattern, a class (the Context) is supposed to behave like different classes depending on its state. The state pattern avoids the use of switch and if statements to change behavior.

```
public interface MobileState {

    public void getState();
}
```

```java
public class Ringing implements MobileState {

    @Override
    public void getState() {
        System.out.println("Mobile is in ringing state");
    }

}
```

```java
public class Silent implements MobileState {

    @Override
    public void getState() {
        System.out.println("Mobile is in silent state");
    }

}
```

```java
public class Vibration implements MobileState {

    @Override
    public void getState() {
        System.out.println("Mobile is in vibration state");
    }

}
```

```java
public class MobileContext implements MobileState{

    private MobileState mobileState;

    public void setMobileState(MobileState state){
        mobileState=state;
    }

    public MobileContext(MobileState mobileState){
        this.mobileState= mobileState;
    }


    public void getState(){
        mobileState.getState();
    }
}
```

```java
public class StatePatternTest {

    public static void main(String[] args) {
        MobileContext ctx = new MobileContext(new Ringing());
        ctx.getState();
        ctx.getState();
        ctx.setMobileState(new Vibration());
        ctx.getState();
        ctx.getState();
        ctx.getState();
        ctx.setMobileState(new Silent());
        ctx.getState();
        ctx.getState();
    }

}
```

Output:

```
Mobile is in ringing state
Mobile is in ringing state
Mobile is in vibration state
Mobile is in vibration state
Mobile is in vibration state
Mobile is in silent state
Mobile is in silent state
```

The benefits of using State pattern to implement polymorphic behavior is clearly visible, the chances of error are less and it's very easy to add more states for additional behavior making it more robust, easily maintainable and flexible. Also State pattern helped in avoiding if-else or switch-case conditional logic in this scenario.

When to use the State Design Pattern:

Use the State pattern in either of the following cases:
* An object's behavior depends on its state, and it must change its behavior at run-time depending on that state.

* Operations have large, multipart conditional statements that depend on the object's state. This state is usually represented by one or more enumerated constants. Often, several operations will contain this same conditional structure. The State pattern puts each branch of the conditional in a separate class. This lets you treat the object's state as an object in its own right that can vary independently from other objects.

State Design Pattern in Java:

* javax.faces.lifecycle.LifeCycle#execute ()

ITERATOR PATTERN

Iterator pattern in one of the behavioral pattern and it's used to provide a standard way to traverse through a group of Objects. Iterator pattern is widely used in java collection framework where Iterator interface provides methods for traversing through a collection.

The logic for iteration is embedded in the collection itself and it helps client program to iterate over them easily. Iterator pattern is not only about traversing through a collection; we can provide different kind of iterators based on our requirements. Iterator pattern hides the actual implementation of traversal through the collection and client programs just use iterator methods. An Iterator object contains public methods to allow a client object to navigate through the list of objects within the container.

Iterator
* Defines an interface for accessing and traversing elements.

ConcreteIterator
* Implements the Iterator interface.

* Keeps track of the current position in the traversal of the aggregate.

Aggregate
* Defines an interface for creating an Iterator object.

ConcreteAggregate

* Implements the Iterator creation interface to return an instance of the proper ConcreteIterator.

When to use the Iterator Design Pattern:

Use the Iterator pattern:
* To access an aggregate object's contents without exposing its internal representation.

* To support multiple traversals of aggregate objects.

* To provide a uniform interface for traversing different aggregate structures (that is, to support polymorphic iteration).

* Iterator pattern is useful when you want to provide a standard way to iterate over a collection and hide the implementation logic from client program.

Iterator Pattern in JDK:

* java.util.Iterator
* java.util.Enumeration

INTERPRETER PATTERN

Interpreter pattern is one of the **behavioral design patterns** and is used to define a grammatical representation for a language and provides an interpreter to deal with this grammar. The best example of this pattern is java compiler that interprets the java source code into byte code that is understandable by JVM. Google Translator is also an example of interpreter pattern where the input can be in any language and we can get the output interpreted in another language.

To implement interpreter pattern, we need to create Interpreter context engine that will do the interpretation work and then we need to create different Expression implementations that will consume the functionalities provided by the interpreter context. Finally we need to create the client that will take the input from user and decide which Expression to use and then generate output for the user.

When to use the Interpreter Design Pattern

Use the Interpreter pattern when there is a language to interpret, and you can represent statements in the language as abstract syntax trees. The Interpreter pattern works best when

* The grammar is simple. For complex grammars, the class hierarchy for the grammar becomes large and unmanageable. Tools such as parser generators are a better alternative in such cases. They can interpret expressions without building abstract syntax trees, which can save space and possibly time.

* Efficiency is not a critical concern. The most efficient interpreters are usually not implemented by interpreting

parse trees directly but by first translating them into another form. For example, regular expressions are often transformed into state machines. But even then, the translator can be implemented by the Interpreter pattern, so the pattern is still applicable.

Interpreter Design Pattern in JDK:

* java.util.Pattern
* java.text.Normalizer
* java.text.Format

MEMENTO PATTERN

Memento pattern is one of the **behavioral design patterns**. Memento design pattern is used when we want to save the state of an object so that we can restore later on. Memento pattern is used to implement this in such a way that the saved state data of the object is not accessible outside of the object; this protects the integrity of saved state data. Memento pattern is implemented with two objects – **Originator** and **Caretaker**. Originator is the object whose state needs to be saved and restored and it uses an inner class to save the state of Object. The inner class is called **Memento** and its private, so that it can't be accessed from other objects.

Caretaker is the helper class that is responsible for storing and restoring the Originator's state through Memento object. Since Memento is private to Originator, Caretaker can't access it and it's stored as an Object within the caretaker.

One of the best real life examples is the text editors where we can save its data anytime and use undo to restore it to previous saved state. We will implement the same feature and provide a utility where we can write and save contents to a File anytime and we can restore it to last saved state. For simplicity, I will not use any IO operations to write data into file.

When to use the Memento Pattern:

Use the Memento Pattern in the following cases:
* A snapshot of (some portion of) an object's state must be saved so that it can be restored to that state later, and

* A direct interface to obtaining the state would expose implementation details and break the object's encapsulation.

Memento Pattern in JDK:
* java.util.Date
* java.io.Serializable

_____End_____

_____

www.ingramcontent.com/pod-product-compliance
Lightning Source LLC
LaVergne TN
LVHW022351060326
832902LV00022B/4374